First Facts

DRAWING
PETS
A Step-by-Step Sketchbook

by Mari Bolte
illustrated by Lucy Makuc

CAPSTONE PRESS
a capstone imprint

First Facts are published by Capstone Press,
1710 Roe Crest Drive, North Mankato, Minnesota 56003
www.capstonepub.com

Library of Congress Cataloging-in-Publication Data
Bolte, Mari, author.
  Drawing pets : a step-by-step sketchbook / by Mari Bolte ; illustrated by Lucy Makuc.
      pages cm. — (First facts. My first sketchbook)
  Summary: "Step-by-step instructions and sketches show how to draw a variety
of pets"— Provided by publisher.
  ISBN 978-1-4914-0281-8 (library binding)
  ISBN 978-1-4914-0286-3 (ebook pdf)
1. Animals in art—Juvenile literature. 2. Drawing—Technique—Juvenile literature. I.
Makuc, Lucy, illustrator. II. Title.
  NC783.8.P48B65 2015
  743.6—dc23   2014013816

Editorial Credits
Juliette Peters, designer; Katy LaVigne, production specialist

Photo Credits
Capstone Studio: Karon Dubke, 5 (photos); Shutterstock: Azuzl (design element),
Kalenik Hannah (design element), oculo (design element)

Printed in the United States of America in North Mankato, Minnesota.
052014   008087CGF14

Table of Contents

Pet Sketch

Kittens and puppies
aren't pets that are new.
But mice, lizards, and fish
like to be drawn too!

Do you love putting pets to paper? Then this book is for you. Follow these tips and the simple steps on each page. You'll be drawing furry, fluffy, or scaly pets in no time.

TIP ① Draw lightly. You will need to erase some lines as you go, so draw them light.

TIP ② Add details. Little details, such as pointy teeth or movement lines, make your drawings more realistic.

TIP ③ Color your drawings. Color can make a cute drawing even more adorable!

You won't need an exercise wheel or
litter box. But you will need some supplies.

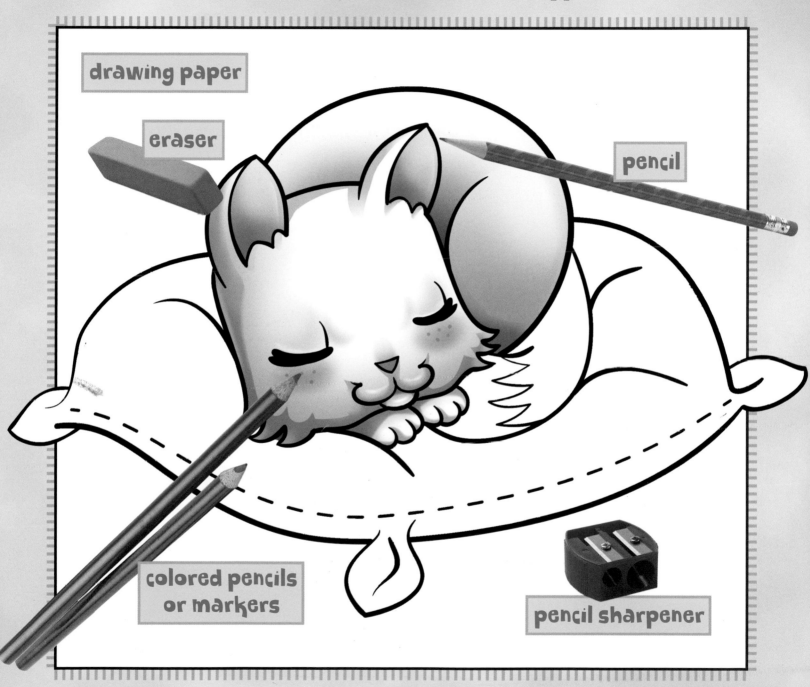

drawing paper

eraser

pencil

colored pencils
or markers

pencil sharpener

Sharpen your pencils, and get ready to draw any
pet you can imagine. It will be a furrily fun time!

Pointing Pup

The search is over for your best friend! Your new pet will be fetching you art supplies in no time.

Final

Draw one curved oval. Draw
a square shape with rounded
edges for the body. Sketch in
lines for the legs and tail.

Don't Forget!
Erase lines that go under
something else. For example,
erase the lines that go through
the dog's head in step 2.

Close the lines you drew in Step 1 to
finish the dog's legs and tail. Add a
rectangle with rounded corners for
the ear and an oval for the eye. Don't
forget the doggy's smile!

Add a curved line for the nose.
Add detail lines to finish the dog's
paws and eye. Add some scalloped
lines for the dog's white spots.

Slithering Snake

Fluff and fuzz aren't for everybody. Scaly snakes are some peoples' favorite pets.

Final

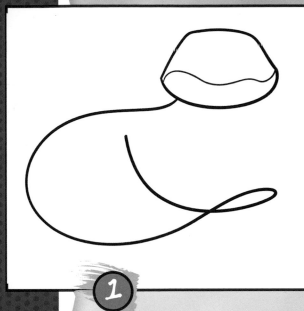

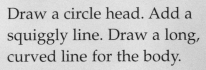

1

Draw a circle head. Add a
squiggly line. Draw a long,
curved line for the body.

2

Add another long, curved line,
and connect it to the other curved
line. Draw two circles for eyes.
Add two curved lines to shape
the bottom of the snake's head.

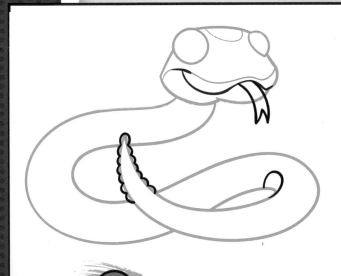

3

Draw a scalloped line around the ends
of the snake's tail. Give the snake a
smile and a tongue. A narrow half-circle
at the bend in the snake's body will
make the body look curved.

4

Add more half circles along the
snake's body. Wide, dark lines
give the snake's eyes life. Add
detail lines to the tail and tiny
dots for the nose.

Friendly Fangs

They aren't the cuddliest, but tarantulas can make great pets! Just don't try to snuggle one!

Final

1

Draw a circle for the tarantula's head. Then draw two half circles for the rest of the body. Add lines for legs.

2

Draw a smile onto the head. Add curved lines to the body. Then add a scalloped line around the end of the spider's body. Add detail lines for the tarantula's legs.

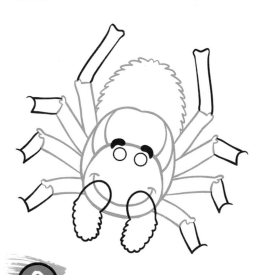

3

Add two fuzzy bean shapes for the spider's fangs. Draw more detail lines on the legs.

4

Add curves for the tarantula's feet and some detail lines on each leg. Draw small circles on the tarantula's head for its extra eyes.

Sleeping Snowball

Shh ... draw quietly! This sweet kitten is taking a catnap. Sketch it now, and pet it later.

Final

1

Draw two circles for the body and tail. Add a bell shape for the head. Then sketch a curved line for a pillow.

2

Add detail lines for the cat's fur, and pointed ovals to make its ears. Then draw in some curved lines for the rest of the pillow.

3

Add detail lines inside the ears. Then add scalloped lines for the cat's paws and mouth. Curved lines show that the cat is sitting on top of the pillow.

4

Add dark lines for the cat's closed eyes. A tiny triangle makes the nose. Zig-zag lines give the cat's tail some color. Dotted lines around the bottom edge of the pillow look like tiny stitches.

Bet It's a Betta

Betta fish are some of the easiest pets out there. They're pretty and don't need a lot of space. Draw a betta in every color of the rainbow!

Final

1

Draw a bean shape for the body. Add two curved lines on the top and two more on the side for the fish's fins. Then draw a wavy line for a mouth.

2

Make the fish's tail with a big half-circle. Add zig-zag lines at the tail's edge. Add more zig-zags inside the tail and back fins. Use more curved lines for another side fin. Use circles and half-circles for the fish's eyes. Finally, draw bubbles for realism.

3

Add a pupil in the center of the fish's eye. Use scalloped lines for scales along the body. Then add detail lines on all the fins. Two small dots make the fish's nose.

Chubby Bunny

Bunnies are becoming more popular as pets. They are playful and easy to train. Draw your dream bunny, and give it a treat to nibble.

Final

1

Draw a circle head. Then draw a round body below the head. Add two long lines for ears. Two circles make the eyes, and a long oval will be the carrot.

2

Add curved lines around the ear lines you drew in Step 1. Use scalloped lines to draw the bunny's feet and legs. Then add a rounded "W" for its mouth.

3

Sketch scalloped lines down the bunny's back. Draw a cloud shape for the carrot top. Add detail lines for the bunny's eyelids, cheeks, and chest. Add teeth and a heart-shaped nose.

4

Draw two circles inside the eyes for pupils. Add detail lines to the carrot and the bunny's nose. Then add its fluffy tail.

Pretty Pony

Yay or "neigh" to a prancing pony?
Vote yes with this miniature horse.

Final

1

Draw a large oval for a body and a smaller oval for a head. Add detail lines for ears, legs, and a tail.

2

Add a triangle to finish the pony's ears. Curved lines make the neck, mane, mouth, and chin. Detail lines give the legs more shape. Draw scalloped lines for the bottom of the pony's legs.

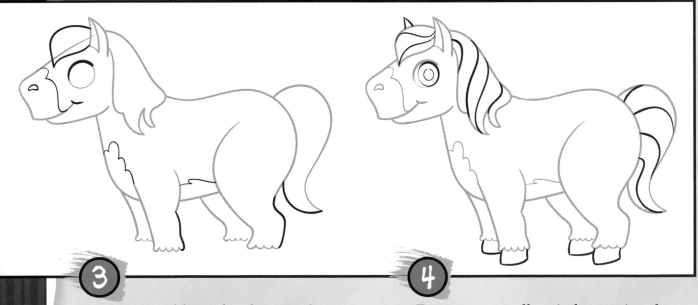

3

Add curved lines for the pony's tail and forelock. Draw a circle for an eye, and a small teardrop for a nostril. Sketch detail lines to finish the legs and scalloped lines for the pony's lighter areas.

4

Draw two smaller circles to give the eye more life. Add four squares for hooves. Detail lines on the mane and tail and a tiny triangle for another ear finish this cutie.

Rat on the Run

Love 'em or hate 'em, there's no doubt that mice and rats can be great pets. Help this critter run the rat race.

Final

1

Draw an oval with slightly pointed ends. Add more pointed ovals for the feet and ear. Then draw a curved line for a tail.

2

Use two large circles to draw the mouse's wheel. Use straight and curved lines to draw an ear. Add another line to the tail. Add curved lines for the back leg and a tiny square for a tooth.

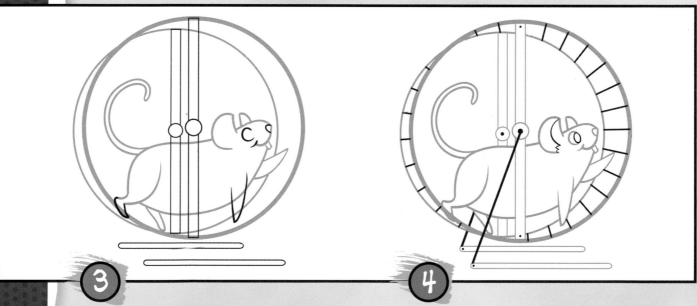

3

Add two long, vertical rectangles at the centers of the circles. Draw small circles in the middle of the rectangles. Add two long lines underneath, for the wheel's base. Sketch a half-circle for the eye. Add detail lines for the nose and legs.

4

Draw dots in the center, bottom, and top of the circle. Then connect the center dots to the base lines underneath. Straight lines will finish the outside of the wheel. Detail lines for the ear and eye will finish off your running rodent.

Loveable Lizard

Lizards are easy to care for and easy to draw! Don't feel like sticking with green? Lizards come in all shapes, sizes, and colors!

Final

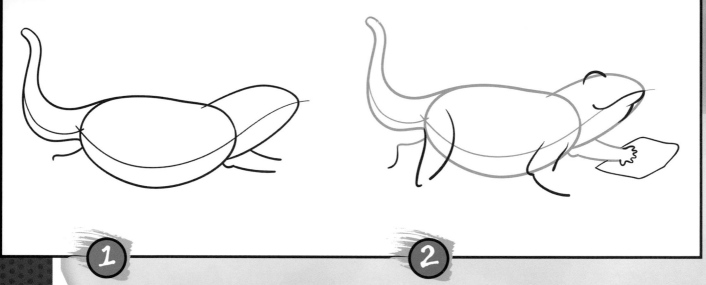

1

Draw an oval for the body. Attach another oval shape for the head. Then add a curved line for a tail. Sketch a detail line for the lizard's stomach. Add small detail lines for the legs.

2

Add curved lines for the lizard's eye, mouth, and legs. Use scalloped lines to give the lizard a foot. Draw a diamond shape for a rock.

3

Sketch a curved line over the top of the lizard's front leg. Draw a scalloped line over the detail line from Step 1. Add an almond shape for an eye. Draw scalloped lines on the other front foot. Then use detail lines to add more rock shapes.

4

Use scalloped lines to give the lizard back feet. Draw a small circle for an ear hole. Add detail lines to give your lizard life. Finish the rocks with more detail lines. Finish the lizard by drawing lines on its belly and tail.

Read More

Bergin, Mark. *It's Fun to Draw Pets*. New York: Skyhorse Publishing Inc., 2014.

Gray, Peter. *How to Draw Cats and Dogs and Other Pets*. How to Draw Animals. New York: PowerKids Press, 2014.

Masiello, Ralph. *Ralph Masiello's Farm Drawing Book*. Watertown, Mass.: Charlesbridge, 2012.

Internet Sites

FactHound offers a safe, fun way to find Internet sites related to this book. All of the sites on FactHound have been researched by our staff.

Here's all you do:

Visit *www.facthound.com*

Type in this code: 9781491402818

Super-cool stuff!

Check out projects, games and lots more at
www.capstonekids.com

24